The Alabaster Box

Poetry by Opal Busbee Staples

Full Circle Publishing
PO BOX 8549
Biloxi, MS 39535
www.juliekeene.com

For information address Full Circle Publishing Rights Department, PO BOX 8549, Biloxi, MS 39535

Printed in the United States of America

First Printing, 2017

ISBN-13: 978-0692943229
ISBN-10: 0692943226

Dedication

This book is dedicated to the thirteen children of Opal Staples and their families, all of her grandchildren and great-grandchildren. May the good memories live on forever. A special thanks to the "Helper" who put order and clarity to papers hidden in notebooks and boxes for many years. Now legible, the poems ring loud and clear as they are lifted from the pages of **THE ALABASTER BOX**.

Acknowledgements

A special thanks to all that have made contributions in any way toward the presentation and completion of this wonderful collection of poems.

To our youngest sister, Vicki Deborah, we express heartfelt gratitude for her labor of love. Countless hours were spent as she orchestrated the orderly arrangement of these poems with a typed print of most of them. One might say that light shone out of darkness, maybe order out of chaos. This book would not have been published apart from the completion of this monumental task. We will be forever grateful for the preservation of these eternal riches that have been passed on to us, our children and friends.

A tribute to the memories of both – the good and tough times – that brought the inspiration to pen these words. May the readers of this book of poems treasure and enjoy it.

TABLE OF CONTENTS

Preface

Preface

A costly and precious oil, rare ointment from her Alabaster Box, was penned as she wrote the poetry shared on the following pages. This inspired volume of poems carries a sweet fragrance of valuable perfume. It has been stated that the alabaster box often times connects the giver to the destiny of the receiver. The experiences of life made the cost of oil in her alabaster box priceless as she poured much of it out on the pages of this book. She was 83 years old when she crossed over to that eternal abode to be with her best friend, Jesus.

So we, the family, say thanks to you, Mom, for passing on this legacy. Our memories of you as **Mother**, a Christian, lady, wife, friend, and writer will live on forever as we read this invaluable collection of poetry entitled, *"The Alabaster Box."*

The Alabaster Box

There was a maid in the long, long ago,
who came to the Master, her devotion to show.
Twas in her possession filled with ointment so rare,
The Alabaster Box that the maiden did bare.
Then she took her possession to the Master's feet,
and anointed our Saviour with the odor so sweet.
"She anointed my burial", the Master declared,
"with the contents of the box which the maiden prepared."

Then said Judas of the long, long ago,
"It's a waste o' money!" And his face was aglow,
with the greed of the money which the love of it brings,
The root of all evil, the lust of all men.
"The poor", said he, "need money this would bring,
to pour it on the ground and to waste it is sin."
That he cared not for the poor, his vile ways did show,
But that the money in his own purse would go.

Looking down at her, the Master did say,
"This shall be remembered for many a day.
Tell all the people of the deed that she did.
She anointed my burial by no one was bid,
and the glory of her head upon my feet was laid,
to wipe up my footsteps was the desire of this maid."

Is your Alabaster Box filled with odors so rare?
Is it filled with the wonderful essence of prayer?
Is your heart filled with feeling so lowly and meek,
to bow before our Master and wipe off his feet?

My Flower Garden

I made a poem with my hoe,
and early every morning I would go
to draw out the lines in a plausable rhythm,
with accents and dashes as they were given.
The lines became rows filled with beauties there,
after daintily spacing them around with care.

The Bride's Wreath and Blue-Bells gently smiled,
as they swayed together down the long aisle.
Alas! For the Bleeding Hearts stopped their to-do,
aisles then became rows where Bachelor Buttons grew.
The Old Maids frowned as they shook their heads,
while the Black-Eyed Susies blinked with dread
at the thought of a last chance for someone to wed.

Prim-Rose lifted her head with pride,
and Perry-Winkle claimed her, the blushing bride.
The Lacy Fern and Violets Blue
made a beautiful row beside the pew.
The Morning Glory looked down about the room,
and the Sunflower consented to accompany the groom.

The Wind sang the march, "Here Comes the Bride".
The Sun Beam danced, the Cloudlets cried.
Can't you see them there?
Many flowers in a row.
This beautiful poem that I made with my hoe.

Leisure

Once in my leisure, I painted a picture with my pen
and ere my pen left the time and the scenes within
as the sound of the writing swept across the page,
like the sound of the strokes that an artist brush made.
My ears received the sound each portrayed.

My paper is a canvas, my pen is a brush.
My words will be drawn with a silvery hush.
Like a sighing whisper in the dearest tone,
as innumerable brooklets go slimmering along.

I painted the stones in the picture within,
creation of melody accosted them.
Embracing the stones, enchanting dear,
was melodious harmony surrounding my ear.

As the water met the stones in laughingly play,
it gently caressed them, then dashed away.
Hide-n-Seek, Peek-a-Boo, it seemed to say
from stone to stone, nature's song portrayed.

My pen quietly traced the course of the brook
to its destiny beside the green grassy nook.
This pool of water having stilled the brook's flow –
mysterious quietness, calm, stillness bestowed.

This picture of the pool, where still waters lie,
lay the sheep resting there, with deep contented sighs.
After grazing at length on the green grassy bed
with the Shepherd watching o're his bountifully fed.

The Shepherd, the great Artist, the great Hand of God,
they all play the part in fields they have trod.
By the great Hand of God, from which wisdom goes –
Painter of all pictures, Savior of all souls.

And though I were blind,
could this scene ever fade?
This beautiful picture
my pen has portrayed.

Seasons of Life

The spring of life is a childhood of baby coos,
ribbons of satin, pinks and blues.
Shrieks of crying as Mother goes by,
Delightful laughter as her steps draw nigh.
The crawls, the scampers, the Hide-n-Seek,
little prayers kneeling at Mother's feet.
The shouts, the cheers, as baseball comes
A big bag of candy for the most home runs.

Summer includes teenagers and a decade or two,
as baby and childhood tactics are through.
Declining down the stairway with joy
is the entrance of a youthful girl or boy.
As a player seeks youthful joys aright,
as a soldier who fights for what he thinks is right.
As a worker accomplishes his worthwhile task,
as a worshiper of God 'til the very last.

Autumn days have come to claim
the matured adult and what he has attained.
Riches of this world, land and gold,
are men's heart treasures – joys untold.

But the man who has lived in his heart desires,
wisdom and knowledge, in close acquaintance with God,
has chosen the best, fine quality is he,
will inherit life abundant and prosperity.

The last work of life, death of winter so cold,
that God prepared to complete the scroll.
Of the full developed life abiding its time,
the great reaper prepares to glean the vine.
So he thrust in his sickle and began to reap,
as command of the trumpet herded the sheep.
And gathered the souls in the bosom of God,
for all to be read at the great judgment bar.

Thoughts

In my mediation and fancies,
I was reveling one day,
When a host of fleeting thoughts
went winging along their way.

I could vision them as great flocks of wild geese
migrating through the air,
and thousands upon thousands of black birds
trying to escape the icy clutches of winter's frosty air.

Some came in formation,
others, here and there.
They filled the air with many specks —
quite a polka-dot affair.

To capture one is my fancy,
to master a thought — my aim.
To harness, dress, and polish it
would greatly be my gain.

So I'll gather my net, my line, hook, and sinker,
and with softness of foot I'll tread.
As a hunter that slips while leaves crush and crinkle,
I'll capture my thoughts with no dread.

With anxiety and patience, I'll array them.
I'll polish and shine them with care.
After much consideration, I'll exhibit them,
for the eyes of the world to ensnare.

When I capture my thoughts, I'll array them
with beauties and gems so rare,
with glory and truth to enfold them
and gird them about with care.

I'll deck them about with jewels of love
linked together with kindness and peace.
Upon clouds of tenderness will float up above
and relax in the sunshine of ease.

Ruffles of purity will enshroud them
on linen so righteous and white.
With honesty always about them
and charity to light up the night.

The higher they sail in virtuous skies
tempered with wisdom and grace,
To flee from evil and wicked paths
with patience to win the race.

Cultured and poised and ready for action,
loaded in literature form,
ready to live in someone's heart
to make a more perfect one.
Thoughts, words, books, and speeches -
all are taking another great ride.
Soap boxes, pulpits, and library tables -
line upon line, there side-by-side.

My Son John

Now Johnny in his boastings was the proud professor.
Not only a professor, but a proud possessor
of wit and charm.
How well he could boast of braun and brain,
regardless of pleasure, joy, or pain.
He delighted to show his strong arm.

Said he to his mother who was a bold reprover,
"You disturb my nice leisure and cause displeasure,
Your words vex me so."
"Nevertheless now, Johnny", said his mother so loud.
"You are mine, and I made you, so don't be so proud."

"Nay", answered Johnny, and showed no devotion –
"God made me big and stout."
God first made nature, so have no great elation.
Evolution in Johnny was only translation
from God to man, no doubt.

Evolution has been disproved since Johnny came,
for a jellyfish has never turned to John's kind of man.
Blood and bones, and flesh of my flesh,
have made my son Johnny
quite happy and blessed.

Sarah

A particle of love was planted once
in a bosomy bed of ole mother earth.
That embryo nestled in the coziest spot
to be fed and warmed as fell its lot.
To abide its time in the snuggest place
then ushered into its own little space.

Lovely imaginations and illusions
caused many a thought and vain conclusion
so plain that the image upon my heart
Was imprinted there never to depart.
The desired bundle of baby days
with perfections of coos and cuddling ways.
Baby boy with dimples and blues
then tiny overalls and tennis shoes.

How I could revel with the thoughts of my mind,
so much desired them and naturally I find
that I could go on pretending
and many thoughts conceive
that the impossible would be reality and not make-believe.

Daily meditation of the hopeful event
brought bountiful feastings to my heart's content.
Food for thought in abounding measure
gave happiness supreme in smiling pleasure.

Regardless which way my mind would travel
that image like a magnet brought me back to reality
those thoughts of a baby boy so cuddly and sweet
with black hair, pink and white, and tiny little feet.

Out of all those illusions so full of sweetness
on which my fated soul still continued in its weakness
which was soon to be the mother of reality so plain
to give birth to facts the truth unfeigned.

Yes, out of these fancies and thoughts so fair
of coos and dimples and black curly hair
came a baby girl so naked and bare,
red and wrinkled and head without hair.

Mother Nature's hand so deftly laid
and wrote up a blueprint of that little maid.
Long, thick hair of exquisite charm,
framing a face, so ardently fond.

As rose buds grow and blossom forth
and Nature's lovely theme unfolds,
unmalicious and unselfish both
a lovable heart of purity molds.

And in our hardened calloused life so aged,
my ears drink in a sweet refrain
"Except Ye become as a little child"
Our Savior's words remain unchanged.

Betty and Gary

Gary was no gossip or tattle, if you please,
but just wanted to tell his mother to set her mind at ease
that a wedding cake was soon to be made.

No one would have talked but at the store, if you please,
Along came the bread man to set his mind at ease,
Was told of a marriage that would never fade.

Said Gary to Bill very worried, if you please,
an announced engagement would set my mind at ease
and make me happy to know it was well nigh on its way.

Now Betty is pretty and sweet, if you please,
for her engagement is announced to set their minds at ease,
and on the lips of every other maid.

I would not have you worry my darling, if you please,
just fix the date real quick to set my mind at ease
then I'll know when you shall be my mate.

Betty was his darling so pretty, if you please,
her mind was made up not to set his mind at ease
And a wedding date was definitely delayed.

Then I'll not see you pouted Gary, if you please,
and won't see you again til you set my mind at ease
with an announcement of a wedding date portrayed.

Now Betty and Gary will get together, if you please,
for absence from one another
will not set their minds at ease
so a wedding date is well nigh on its way.
So togetherness is much needed, if you please,
one mind and one accord will set their mind at ease
And a beautiful wedding will never decay.

The Cross

This cross that I bare, why is it there,
these thorns that prick and stick and make me weep?
Why do I have to bare this, Lord, that tears me into shreds
and makes me seek for an easy path
that will not leave the solitude of peace?
Thy load is mine for Thou art mine and I am thine.
Thy load is mine and will be mine until Thou
tears thyself apart.
No more shall a selfish wave of pity o're me roll,
for all I can do is to help to share some dear one's load.

As I look into the sanctuary of memories
that have hidden themselves between the
shadows of time,
I can see a tall, straight, holy figure
silhouetted against the back of my mind.

That figure is the One I will follow,
no more will I murmur, no more will I complain,
for that figure of Jesus is written there
indelibly plain.
How willingly He suffered, though not too bodily strong
with power and might.

They hid their faces with no esteem to be given,
choosing darkness rather than light.

Afflicted and smitten of God was He
no pleasant view to the eyes of the natural man.
But his willingness to carry somebody's cross
was more beautiful than any other plan.
Upon his frail shoulders was all sin laid,
and a scapegoat for all ages He became.
So Jesus is the one that will carry your cross,
but in return we must do His command.

Heaven's Refrain

Some dream of owning planets,
some dream of owning moons,
having power over inhabitants
in palaces of many rooms.

In my heart there's a great big room
holding my heaven for me
Since Jesus came in and turned it to gold,
tis abode of angelic company.

They sing and they play on their golden harps.
Their presence brings ecstasies rare.
The joys of a Savior can never be told,
the reward of a cross he had to bare.

They are mine and I cherish them greatly,
I clutch them very fast.
For my heart must contain all the love it can hold
and rejoice with the heavenly guests.

No hate, no grudges, no covetous thoughts
can mingle with the Savior's guests.
Harmony and beauty cannot be obtained
if defiled by a smear or a jest.

No scorn, no mocking, no gossip can remain,
No hint of a stubborn look.
For all must be pure in heaven's refrain,
To be a song in the angels' book.

Whiter Than Snow

I didn't mean to fall, Lord,
in this puddle hole of sin.
I didn't mean to mingle
with the group of drunken men.
But thou, O Lord, has pulled me out
of mire into the Light.
Soap and water just out of Heaven
will make me clean and white.

Get your soap and water, Lord,
for I am dirty and black.
And a wash rag like mom used
yes, that's a fact.
Now, wash me, Lord, my head
my hands, my heart.
Make me clean as I can be, Lord,
and from you, I won't depart.
And get the mud all out of my eyes, Lord,
so I can plainly see.
Lord, you know I want to be holy,
just like thee.

When I was a little ole boy
playing around with the other fellows,
I'd hear mom say, "Now don't get dirty son.
Don't be so helter-skelter."
And it would turn out in the end
that I'd be the goat,
and I'd be in the blackest mud hole
almost up to my throat.
Then mom would pull me out with
a scowl as you know,
and I'd say real quick,
"Wash me, and I shall be whiter than snow."

The First Day

Darkness!
And God said, "Let there be Light."
And then His word displayed
The light then came
A huge projectile in the sky,
With gleaming rays flashing like meteorites
Which did defy the thick bleak darkness.

Thick, black darkness covered the land,
The Sea, the air; and every man.
Packed and compressed on Him around,
Like shackles of steel that had Him bound.
Then a shaft of lightening formed,
And His great hand with a two edged sword
Seemed to expand and enlighten the heart
And life of man.

The trail of the jagged rippling rays,
Split through the darkness as a battle ablaze
From Heaven to Earth as one amazed,
The battle immortal was in His gaze
Why! And behold! The darkness
Was driven within a span.

One bright round shining sphere
Directly overhead did place,
And drove the darkness far beyond,
As it danced from space to space,
Inch by Inch down the compass path
It chased the darkness from the orbital goal,
Always to the west, then hour by hour,
One, Two, and at the point of six
Completed the beginning of the day in its roll.
And on and on the day ensued
As the battle kept raging on
Until the light retraced its step,
Thus forming the rising Dawn.

On and on the battle raged
From midday sun to western phase,
Light fought the darkness
Ere we must gaze
With fond delight
And ere our ears received with care
The words of God. Come nigh, Come say
"The evening and the Morn were the first day",
For all the people to rejoice and pray.

As the Sun in the sky wrought for the day,
So the Son of God drives the darkness away,
And the Light of the knowledge of the glory of God,
Will shine in our hearts to stay.

Adam and Eve

Adam and Eve once lived in a garden,
The trees were their home and God was their father,
His loads were easy and the burdens were light,
His tasks were few and his commands were right.

Innocence and ignorance for a blissful repose
For they didn't know that nudity was exposed,
Until command of the Lord came into his ear,
Hearken to my voice, refuse not to hear.

Eat not of the tree in the midst of the garden,
Hearken to my voice or I'll never pardon,
Judgment shall come and give birth to death,
Which has never existed on Earth as yet.

So Adam and Eve ate the delicious food,
Of the trees in the garden where they stood.
And the trees in the midst of the garden there
Were loaded with fruit so palatable and fair.

The command of the Lord was in Adam's heart,
and wisdom desired it to never depart,
Eve persuaded Adam and he transgressed,
The wisdom in his heart, Adam had to confess,
Departed at the sound of the tempters jest.

God came walking in the cool of the day,
Oh! Adam! Where Art Thou? He hastened to say,
Adam and Eve both lost their composure
And hid behind a tree to cover their exposure.

Guilt and shame covered Adam and Eve,
As God's word came penetrating through the trees,
Tend the Commandment which was ordained to life,
Adam found unto death filled with wars and strife.

Once he was alive without the law,
Happy and contented, in the garden aglow,
With the love of the father his heart did bestow,
The glory of paradise as a river did flow.

God's commandment came for the good and the best,
But rejecting God's word he found unto death.
Old Satan and sin, known as the serpent then,
Deceived, and took up his abode within.

So Ole Satan took up his abode within
And made Adam a very good servant of sin,
When he would do good, Satan made him stop,
And evil was there, whether wanted or not.

He was dead to God's word but alive to sin,
Bound and compelled by The Evil Within.
Oh wretched man who can deliver,
From this body of death? Oh God leave me never!

So Ole man Adam had to die out to sin
And again serve the true one to have Grace within,
Jesus the righteous one who hung on the tree,
Gives Grace to fallen ones and restores eternally.

At Adam's disobedience many died,
In the righteousness of Jesus, they can now abide,
Instead of sin's fig leaves so brittle and brisk,
The robe of his righteousness, they will now be blessed.

The old serpent is not the right kind of thing,
To fill our lives with Satan and sin,
His deceitful boasts have none of it,
For he is a liar and the father of it.

Silent Fall
(or Snow)

Did you ever hear the silent fall,
In the lulled deep darkness of the slumbering night?
Like the hovering cling of a countless call,
To invade in silence its own natural rights.

The Gentle Touch, the caressing stroke,
Nature's snug enclosures of Ole Mother Earth,
So silent, so harmless, yet this invasion,
Captures heart, soul, and body at its persuasion,
Makes us to laugh, to love, enjoying its seclusion,
To dance with the children's confusion
While they gather with joy icicle profusion,
They could last no length at the Snows conclusion.

The Joy, the love, the laughter, the shouts,
A continuous display as the Master pours out
Of his cup of Love upon every house
Indentured with joy routing each pout.

Upon every street though spotted and stained,
And country roads filled with the wounded and slain,
Of the flowers and brambles, and bushes and grass.
They've collapsed in heaps and every eye that passed,
Moaned the fact their die was cast.

Creeping in filtering and covering with white,
All the dead and mutilated quite hidden from sight.
By the blanket of snow,
So beautiful and white,
untrampled without a smear or a blight.

As it goes, we have made an intolerable show,
Our sins, as it were, all filthy and so-
God, with his love has washed us clean,
Whiter, yes whiter, than an Earthly scene.

Take heed lest we trample the blood with its flow,
Which has cleansed every stain,
Made us love every foe-
And changed our hearts from a worldly beat,
Relaxing with angels at Jesus feet.

Scars and Traces

The scars and the traces, and the lines on the faces,
Show days of misery, of grief and woe,
To me, there is beauty in the harshness there,
For sorrow had softened the soul, made it fair.
The fingers of grief etched the picture with care,
And perfection stamped it plainly ever so rare.

The God of all Graces, and the king of all races,
Has opened a window to the depth of the Soul.
To me all emotions are measured there,
Reflected and mirrored, enchantingly fair,
The virtues of the Soul brought forth with care,
Like diamonds and rubies, yes, ever so rare.

The traces of Tears, falling down throughout the years,
Have written a design that spring out from the soul.
To me its Graces have been bought with a price,
Tempered and tried once, twice, and thrice,
Until rich gold truly it suffices
The Potter himself, being Jesus the Christ.

Never Put Off Until Tomorrow
(What Should Be Done Today)

Once I was alive, ambitious and Young,
Harboring a fancy Just for Fun-
Illusions and Daydreams to flood my day,
Air castles like bubbles to float away.

How badly I wanted them there to stay,
Clutching them close don't leave me I pray,
And grasping them lightly till maturity comes,
Was the hardest task but had to be done.

Alas! And alack! They faded and died
And try as I would, no more could I hide
Disappointments that come when dreams wilt away
Dwindle and die at the close of the day.

I can think of the beauties that are murdered and slain
By cruel deceit, but despair takes the blame,
Layers and layers and loads upon loads
They came to crush that beautiful rose.

The songs I created that sounded to the Stars,
The Melody of Angels on the Musical bars.
The poems, the prophecies, the philosophies of Life
were born, then doomed by Wars and strife.

One peek in the casket of devilish Goons,
Nailed down the cover to seal their Doom,
Only a crack which hope chanced to see,
And rebuked the small imps of adversity.

If ever this poem had a moral to learn,
It is to do it today before tomorrow comes.
Your Ambitions, your Visions, your heart's desires,
Should be nurtured, then cared for, before they expire.

The Quail and the Dove

Stepped side by side
Down the long isle of the corridor.
From the homeroom comes the "snickered" sounds,
While some of them were aghast
And some of them were "Horrors".

"The spelling test" came the snickered quote,
Could never have ended with an "O",
And the candidate's pen,
With the "Master's degree"
Said, "O" meant only
"Zero".

The spelling test was not dismissed
It was quietly and strictly discovered,
As the quail reviewed all the spelling rules,
Especially the ones that were troubled.
Add the letter "E" with the "S"
Would only mean definition and Plural
Expansion.

No one wants just one potato,
When dealing with "fries"
"chips" and "Bakes"
Who wants a "Zero" "trouble mix"
On the record of a candidate's space.

All you have to do is to go by the rule,
To make the "Zero"turn into "s s s" es',
Every time you eat a potato
Either "Chip", "fries" or one that you love.
As the rule adds "e-s" to your Potato
Also high points to
"Quail" and to "Dove".

The Sea, The Sea

The Sea, the Sea, The Motherly Sea,
How we do frolic and laugh with glee,
As the warm waves tumble and roll o're me,
In the lap of the Motherly Sea.

The Sea, the Sea, the Fickle Sea!
One like a mother it amuses me,
Those long wavy arms encircle me,
I am tutored and cared for by the Gentle Sea.

The Sea, the Sea, the Fearful Sea!
Long arms like tentacles reach after me,
The tempest and billows rise heavily
And dash together in the Mooring Sea.

Once She's my Mother and Once She's my Judge,
Now in her bosom am I tucked in quite snug.
Now in the air am I dashed above,
The impulsive and impetuous sea.
Ceases to be a mother to me.
Now she will rob me of leisure and play,
This Frantic Sea with her spews of dismay.

Look! Look! This Fickle Sea,
Becomes an angry enemy,
Sunny leisure leaves and brings dismay,
Teaching fun-loving souls they should kneel and pray.

Ah! Parental, Reckless and Changeable Sea!
So fearful are the thoughts that torment me,
To be swirled and churned, I make a plea
Please, my dear Mother, don't deceive me.

But the Angry Sea would not hear my plea,
But belched and heaved quite drunkenly,
Fuming and foaming great sprays misty white,
Now to rest in her arms is an awful plight,
Happy hours on the Sunny beach,
Turn to agony and fear as waving arms reach.

Now, why would the loving mother suddenly turn,
To an angry rebuke no one would spurn?
And the horrible waves dashed high against the shores,
To destroy an evil playhouse which had so many doors.

Some people who are evil will abuse the kind Mother,
With evil wicked ways which cause her to shudder.
One sign, "No cursing", No drinking", No smoking
allowed!
Should be placed at every seashore
To convince every crowd.
That God's divine plan should never be neglected.
Nor His great commandments ever be rejected,
That the work of His Hands might ever be
Stamped plainly upon my memory.

The Sea! The Sea! The beautiful Sea!
No more a resort for the Devil to Score,
But lies peacefully along a God-given shore.

Hands

Cleanse your hands ye sinners,
And humble yourselves
Purify your hearts you double-minded,
Oh, humble yourselves.

Draw nigh to God and He
Will draw nigh to you,
Humble yourselves in the
Sight of the Lord
And He will lift you up.

I would that men would pray
All the way.
Lifting up Holy Hands
No wrath no doubting,
Will enter in Me
I must escape the sinking hands.

To humble our hearts and cleanse our hands,
With things ourselves have "dandled",
The word of God, so pure, so true,
Our searching hearts have handled.

Autumn

A beautiful blanket of Gold, Brown, and Yellow,
Has covered the earth, even every flower,
Autumns cool fingers have deftly laid,
The crisp, crisp, coverlet which timely fades.

The wind played the fiddle and the leaves rocked and
rolled,
The whirl wind picked them up in a whirly – jig float,
And placed them about checkered here and there,
In a design so enchanting, a pattern so rare,
To cover the earth no more naked and bare.
Said I in my heart, "why not take a peek."
For up under the coverlet lays the daintiest sheet,
Of the smoothest softness of downiest fluff.
Of petal sweetness, of flowery stuff.
My eyes beheld the most beautiful fare,
Flowery substance strewn everywhere.

Rose petals of white edged about with red,
The yellows and pinks filled their place in the bed.
Borders of lilac leaves and touch-me-nots too,
Had to be covered and hidden from view.
When things are ready and quietly disposed,
For that beautiful white spread madam winter composed,
With tassels of icicles which hang here and there,
With glittering diamonds when the sun peaks and stares,
The first touch of winter is everywhere.

Looking all around us we can plainly see,
That the flowering petals of springly breeze,
And then the bright coverlet of autumn leaves,
And then snowy bed spread of wintery freeze.
That come very timely one by one,
Though swift be the day from sun to sun.

See, save the Son

See, save the Son
And he to whom the Son will
Reveal him.

No man sees me with
The natural eye
For I am from the spiritual realm.
To obtain my Great rest-
You must cease from the flesh
And enter into the
Kingdom of God.

You cannot see -
My kingdom
From the natural eye must depart
Consider my throne,
Which I alone
Will inhabit within thine heart.

Observe the great Heaven
We're searching
Which lies with in the
Kingdom of God
With your heart for His throne
And your life all His own
For endless ages and odds.

Walking with Jesus in golden serenity,
Like crossing the great sea dryshod
An adoration I'm sending,
Is my soul lowly bending?
Reverently fearing my God?

I trudged this broad-way heavy-laden
Weary, no rest for my soul.
I died out to sin-
Let Jesus come in-
And I'm living a new life with Him
Which lies in the
Kingdom of God

Goodbye

Good-by- A dear ole '83
The Master chose to close its portals
Carefully bowed in eternity
To blend its substance among immortals.

At each obesience where ending has come
With agreed "well done" or with regret,
To exalt the good things summed
Degredate the things beset.

No longer could ole '83
Encroaching, along a brothers rights,
Blocking the streets and pathway of time,
Exploding the mete of days and nights.

So marching on in an orbit's trace,
The moon, the stars, and the sunsets daze,
They sped everyone as the maker prepared
Nor lingered to check on their by-gone days.

And through the escalating days of time,
Always searching to combine,
As onward, upward, we do climb,
And leave the by-gone years behind.

Ascending to the highest level,
There stands the door we seek to find
Everlasting-entrance seems to beckon
And bid us taste His heavenly wine.

Jesus We Would See

The three wise men
with an upward glance
at the Heavenly Body
as it slipped into view
down the Milky Way
it traveled afar
that beautiful bright
shining Eastern Star.

Reaching its designation
sending forth its rays
over the Abode
where Jesus lay,
with Direction and guidance
wise men won't fall
if they let it beckon
give heed to its call.

Others sought Jesus
in divers ways,
Nicodemas by night-
no suspicion was raised-
for a master and teacher
could never be abashed
a visit from a man
of low -bred class
" for " thought he,

his opinion I claim
for God must surely
honor his name
notable Mercies
would nay have been done
by the signs the wise
are securely won.

Then certain Greeks
to The Feast had arrived
"sirs" Jesus we would see
For to worship him we indeed did come
and to see his glorious Ministry
Philip was first to hear his word
and to carry it abroad
and with Andrew they then agreed
to tell it to the Lord.

The words of the wise
are as goads and nails
fastened by masters of assemblies,
to one Shepherd give
to those that desire to find Him; and
life Everlasting.

Rejection Lesson

One healthy urchin -- Stallwart lad
just entering the door of 'teenage fad'
13 years well-nigh on his head-
stood squarely on his broad feet viewing his dad.

"Well, Dad here I am just a looking you o'er,
thinking how nice it would be in your store,
for the shirt on the rack is the toughest yet,
you bet yore boots we've got it to get.

Pee-Wee's got one the toughest thing,
Will skim o're Hills-when you give it a fling,
It'll ne'r wear out regardless of sling-
A Bulldogs Holt won't hurt a thing.

And the toughest britches you ever saw,
Has Peewee got in connection,
They're just like leather-there you are,
What a happy real tough collection.

You can climb up trees and skin a cat,
Cut a flip turn around backward,
Never a stitch and never a tear,
Shows us they'll Shore pass inspection

Ah, come on now dad- I can't see a thing
But must have them in my possession,
For them real tough britches and old leather shirt,
Must never be a rejection.

But Dad in his wisdom smilingly knows
That the shirt and Leather Britches suddenly grows,
Old with possession and constant wear,
And little boy's bodies will again be quite bare.

It's up to dad to do the best he can,
For he knows that clothes never make the right man
Whether silk, satin, or plain corduroy,
Dad will do his part for his own little boy.

O Dawn of Day

Oh! Dawn of day! How pure you are,
Evening and morning have begotten you,
And mothered you with their tender Care.
Atmospheric waves have cherished you
And wrapped you about with freshness so rare.
Great drops of Dew have washed you
And blessed you with a saintly baptismal air,
a newborn babe brought forth twas as nature prepared.

Oh! Dawn of day! The lovely you!
Adorned with the fading Twilight so richly trimmed,
within edging of ruby red,
a Rosy Hue to violet blue,
as thicker clouds obscure the view,
and the flickering waves of the Rising Sun
seem to beckon and wave at the fleeting Dawn.

Oh! Dawn of day! Invigorating.
To inhale your Purity, to taste your sweetness,
makes life worth living.
New Strength is generated by your beautiful creation
your short-lived presence is penetrating,
and makes one glad to Live Another Day.

Oh! Dawn of day! Stimulating!
How well you have played your part.
How well you have mastered your aim,
a beautiful Prelude!
A wonderful beginning!
is the dawn of another day!

Complex

Nothing am I
Nothing have I ever been
Come from nothing
Nothing has ever proven a friend.

Empty am I
Empty will I ever be
Empty as a bottomless tin
That has been battered by many a wind.

Nothing - a vast emptiness
A dismal reality
A blank scroll
Which slowly unrolls
To awaken mortality
Or under the surface
Lies morbid brutality
Intertwined with carnality
Becoming reality.

Nothing-void and Bare
scattered everywhere
like hot white sand
on a burning desert,
a Barren womb
an empty field
ah, who would care
it seems a snare
and no one can barely
utter a prayer.

Hair

long hair
black hair
straggled hair
hair , hair
everywhere

Underneath
a pale face
blushing grace
abashed and abased
by an interlude
(be not so rude)
Regardless combing
hairlets roaming
grooming ceases
a tangled mass
a gruesome task
Remained unfinished

a monotone
(I know you desire to be alone)
droning on
routine Perfection
professional protection
instructional suggestion
a questionable rejection
a rhythmic routine
a complete scene

down the back
everywhere
this hair
mussed hair
teased hair
well set hair
Gaudy streaked and black
blue hair
long hair
a glory to her
beloved, beware
cut it if you dare!

Visit

A visit to the shores on a bright Fair Day,
observance of the Waves as people group to play,
the roar's resoundingly waves rise so high,
accosting the shores which returns a reply.
Sound and Resound, the roar's reach the sky,
as they groaned and roared which the waves did defy;

once Jesus stood there telling ever so bold,
about perilous times wrecking people's Souls.

Yawning Clock

The yawning clock's hands,
tried to cover its face
at the hour of eight,
while the mocking cuckoo,
repeated its chant, not
a whit too late,
the report sounded clear on
lingering ear
that had waited not late.

The Sleep clock's face
so fatigued with its pace;
to complete the race,
arriving on time
agreeing with the Chimes,
of the Cuckoo's date,
while Grandpa clock
across the hall entered the gait.

The little alarm clock entered the race,
to scream it's alarm with all clock mates,
the singing of the Cuckoo's
and Grandpa's dong, dong,
the screaming of the brass
promoted quite a song.

Don't be too late
don't wait too , late,
all the clocks report,
pointed to a date,
they are accurate and consistent,
take a brief estimate.
Profit by their example,
success will be your fate.

Millions of Thanks

Millions of thanks for the millions of things,
you have done for me dear Lord.
Millions of words of sweet Accord ring out so tenderly.
Millions of blessings, which have flowed
Through The Years,
healed millions of heartaches,
wiping millions of Tears
By Jesus the wisdom of God.

Millions of desires , to stronger grow,
causing millions of prayers by which
strength flows,
from Jesus the strength of God.

Proverbial Comment

Passions Run High
and are commonly mixed,
in a habitual dwelling.
Sentimental sighs,
and are tortured or blessed
by unusual meddling.
Kindred live right,
together they are fixed,
yay or nay, they are willing.
Friendship is bright,
and anchors alight
for those not deceiving.
Temptations abide,
here and there it hides
in darkness there lurking.
Patience is nigh
no more sobs and cries,
for a soul that is trusting.
An uneventful life,
considers it plight
and for virtues keep searching.

Gracious

As the rain dropped down with gentle Grace,
upon the uplifted form of an eager face,
when hungry soul willed with fervent desire,
to be richly attired with covet style,
of the loving heart of God's open space,
of a Christian Child in a great human race,
with the Heavenly attire of God's holy word,
wrapped around our hearts in perfect Accord.

As bees in a swarm and ants in a nest,
as a symphony of wild geese displays overhead,
wild beauties of rhyme and Praise in the day,
as they sway with one another,
in their own gracious way.

As Ophrah land of Cloudy Lanes,
the dark grey cloud from which they go,
with icicles daggers in the hand of foe,
far away was a shimmering pose,
a shaft of light - sunlight a glow,
a lake sends its dream of lilies in pairs,
and beautiful summer dream of geese in the air.

The clouds burst forth into massive Rays,
leading the fear-laden geese astray,
fear of icicles, clouds, Those that blow,
Which could ice their wings with none to control.

Flying and sweeping and swaying along,
so beautifully, thrilling very much like a song.
So are we on whom the master bestows,
His Marvelous power to beset the foe,
we sing to the master as his blessings unfold,
Praising Him eternally for a God filled soul.

Mother Nature's Trick

To think that mother nature pulled a freak
as if we should be so awake while thus we sleep,
and Summers warm and Sunny Rays
bring forth the clothes of which we fitly gaze.
And Sun Shines glare through summer days,
old Nature's trick upon the stage,
to find her children drooping with the heat;
for in full dress not so petite,
which thus did increase with the hot summer heat,
her hottest days made them quite complete.

So in full dress wrapped with sultry heat,
they did droop and dwindle in sheer defeat.
Wilted and worn and heavy-laden,
crushed and flushed like a weary Maiden,
old nature comes in her Autumn jest,
to take away their heavy dress.

And then as colder days do come
undress those children one-by-one,
some will heed some disobey
please do not take our clothes away,
we are cold and we want them there to stay,

So choosing and fussing and blowing about,
a wrestle and a whirl they went right out.
Flinging away downward they went a-route,
though, freakish and freezing Mother Nature blows,
they almost froze without their clothes.
Instead of warmth covered Head to Toes,
they stood there with Twigs instead of red nose,
Bleak and bare, they seemed to stare,
in Winter's Icy glare.

Overcoming

Where is the glory of overcoming,
If all temptations are gone?
T'is not he who attains the pedestal
Who, being sheltered from storm and wind
Not soiled, nor stained, nor trampled,
By great or petty sin;
But he who can rise from muck to the skies
From ditch and from gutter as lofty words utter,
"Repent" let me be thy guide.
He that can rise from strife and quarrel
Tis he that can win and attain the laurel
This glittering goal; a prince so royal, a child of the king.

Where is the man, woman or child,
Sunken and degraded being defiled?
One look at the king lifted high on the cross
Will rise above ruin, a triumphant cost.

So the man who overcomes receives the glory
Yes, ore all temptations that come,
Be it fiery trials or stormy seas,
Can always hear the words
"My child" well done.

Prayers

Oh where do they go? Those prayers that I pray each night
What do they do? But banish all fear and strife,
I whisper those words of comfort and love so wise,
And brush back each tear which gathers to dim my eyes.

My prayers are ascending, and upward they go-
Those blessings descending, makes my heart all aglow.
Oh! Heaven's acceptance, brings the Savior's Assurance
each time
Complacent emotion with Godly devotion Sublime,
As the powerful possession of the savior's blessings I feel
Makes the grand reception of heartfelt confession so real .

Uplifted face on bended knee so low
Amazing Grace, How Sweetly the Sound softly flows.
Angelic puriors melodious streams soft and low
A great fiery presence as the glory clouds cover me o're.

Those prayers that I pray
An anguished soul entreats,
For a place of redemption
So infinitely sweet.

Oh where do they go?
Those prayers that I pray each night,
What do they do?
They banished all fear and strife.

My Wondrous God

My Wondrous God!
You dandled the oh so great ocean,
In the palm of your almighty hand.
And Scattered the oh, so small grainlets,
Which painted the shores, of whitest sand.
When wisdom oh so sweetly smiled
At the forming of the pearls so low,
Which dotted the satin Shoreline,
that only the master could cause to grow,
and cloaked it with beauty.
I Marvel at the infinite greatness,
of my wondrous God.

God's love for Fallen Man

God planted the stars and reaped the twinkles,
The beautiful expression of Heaven's love.
Peace and happiness are wedged in each wrinkle
Of lines on the face which shines from above.

God's eyes are the Stars which are filled with twinkles,
As he watches the wondrous things of the night,
Then suddenly those eyes become Misty blinkles
As he blinks back the tears which dim the soft Twilight.

Those tears from God's eyes drop heavily downward,
As he looks upon the things his hands have made,
And the glistening Moon beams dance softly forward,
On the dewy tears that remain unshed.

When the Twilight Fades into early Dawning,
When the breaking of day drives the Moonbeams away,
And the baby sunbeams Frolic in the morning,
With the Masters tears, what a beautiful display.

The grass and the leaves in the limbs of the trees,
Have gathered together those Jewels so rare,
Then the more brilliant sunbeams hastily Breeze,
To gather the tears out of the earth's Mossy hair.

So ole father sun will dry up the tears,
That have fallen during the night,
because of the evil and wicked things,
that lurk in the shadow of Dusky Twilight.

Pain and Agony together with tears
show God's love for a sinful man.
The crown of thorns! Great drops of blood!
Reveal his great Redemptive plan.

Is God Dead?

On bended knee, uplifted in face
With hands clasped tightly upon the breast,
A teardrop glistens, shimmers down
Tells a story, words can't expound
Meek and contrite the gracious Lord
Our hearts so filled with sweet Accord
Cannot despise, His blessings flow
When all the soul is humbled low.

The scoffer looks; one first thought,
To laugh, to jeer, to taunt, to mock,
The foolish fellow, why Fret? He says
"to pray to a god they say is dead?"
The fool in his heart has said about God
"there is not one who started this rot?"
And he knew in his heart that God was not dead.

Those Bended Knees, those tears that streamed,
on the uplifted face sent forth a gleam
of gleaming glory to the foolish man
Who fought against God and the righteous land.
Giving homage to God he makes his plea,
A right Spirit Lord, please let me depart
from evil ways, give me a clean heart.

To Be Like You

Often times there are things I'd like to do,
But to be like you is my choice though friends be few,
No matter where I go in this wide world
I choose to be true,
To the one who died on Calvary- His will I'll do,
Jesus Christ, my Lord, I know your word is true,
Every prayer I make, every breath I take is to be like you,
Repenting of sinful pleasure to be like you,
Casting out Satan's bondage to be like you.

There are other people who would like to know,
that the savior's love on falling man, he would bestow,
that the peace of God might rain in every heart,
that the only source of lasting peace can God impart.
Changing all adamic nature just to be like you
reaching upward through God's Beauty just to be like you.
You are the only One my God to make things true,
every prayer I say,
from an aching soul I pray just to be like you.

There are other places I'd like to go,
through the many places victims sink below,
but the path My Savior trod - very narrow.
He'll Lift us up -he loves us better than the sparrow.
Leaving all Earthly treasure just to be like You,
taking up the cross of Calvary -oh, to be like You!
Jesus Christ, my God, I know you'll lead us through
every prayer I pray each moment of each day,
is to be like You!

Jesus

Jesus a name which we need to call on,
to make one target to Heaven's Glory.
Mortal adjacent to immortality;
Proficient; consistent;
energizes ;accelerates ,
both heart and soul.
Mortal to acquaint with the Heavenly goal,
ignites the tongue to publicize.
Edicts in breverity and longitude.
The Heavenly Supernatural altitude
a derivative of magnificent name
Jesus, Emmanuel,
may God With Us be the same.

If Jesus were a verb, we would conjugate.
If he were a word, we would Define,
he is our Lord, we will elaborate,
laud the potentate.

Exhilarating our voices in highest shrieks,
applauding our Lord from the highest peaks,
tis not natural Mount Airs we accelerate,
But spiritual mounts we can't obliterate.

Looking Backward

A sinner, then saint, then sinner again should never be,
though footsteps fall
from feet that swiftly run into Mischief
though the Savior calls.

Those feet, they track then track again,
should never be, through the savior's blood.
They trample the blood, yes there they trod,
though the savior loves.

Lot's wife looked back, remember her plight,
Should never have been
though the angel warned
Her love for Sodom caused her to turn
To a pillar of salt, as the great sculptor formed.

Look forward not backward, look forward again,
Should never be; so onward we plod,
"for he that putteth forth his hand
to the plow and looketh back
is not fit for the kingdom of God."

Laughter in Heaven

I hear much laughter in heaven,
much joy, much happiness, much praise,
the Angels sublimely rejoicing
for a sinner that is saved by grace.

How much more rejoicing in heaven,
over Sinners when from sin they repent,
Than the Lord's High congregation,
who have joined in the Angel's feast.

The joy of a soul saved From The Snare,
of Satan's glamorous detection,
radiates from afar,
God's Spirit-filled Saints of perfection.

Thousands upon thousands around the king,
present a picturesque scene,
Thousands upon thousands around the throne,
shouting and singing the song of the redeemed.

The glory clouds burst forth,
make rainbows bow
with their colorful Hues,
the Thousand attendants
of The Golden Throne,
who sees a grandeur view?

The melodious laughter Rings true Delight,
upon Sanctified ears that are saved,
their heart vibrates, for a soul has been freed,
Satan lost his last chance to enslave.

Who is at the Door?

Who is at the door, waiting near,
asking for entrance, what is the sound I hear,
graciously the sounds keep falling, why not open for me,
please hear me calling,
and I will live with thee.

Who at my door is knocking
Shivering, bare feet, blue,
pale with the gaunt look of hunger,
bleeding, almost tearing your heart in two.
Standing there with a grief-stricken look,
Will you help me a tear flooded voice softly said
instantly another voice was spoken,
That great voice by which we are led.

I was once at your door standing,
"You gave me no food nor bread."
How gave we, you no food dear Master?
How gave we, you no warm cozy bed?
I came to you cold, hungry, bleeding,
I came as a small helpless lad —
in so much as you did it to the least of these
my bretheren
You have treated me equally as bad.

Who is at my door there begging?
Standing there naked, alone.
Within there relaxed the rich man,
While poor Lazareth smothered a groan.
No clothes, no home, no loving care,
there he stood all covered with sores,
dining with the dogs and grabbing a crumb
And anxiously awaiting more.

The Greatest Reason for Christmas

To the many homes on hills and plains,
This Christmas day is not in vain.
His great message of "Peace on Earth"
Fills every heart with heavenly mirth.

This Christmas day of every age
Should come from a heart
That's richly engraved,
The peace of God forever flows
Redemptive plan conquers every foe.

The day will come not too far hence,
When every heart will be content
When the Savior's lofty hand of Gold
Erases sin and saves the soul.

The Hand That Is Blessed

The hand that is held stretched out to the needy,
Be it bountiful, running over or less,
That hand is beloved by the eager expectants,
That hand is the hand that is blessed.

All the little children hang up their stockings,
In rows, for the forthcoming guest,
When he comes he smiles, then tears fill his eyes;
For their love for the hand that is blessed.

Though many years have aged o'er life
Still our hearts are anticipating,
And memory treasures- not a stocking,
But a great big box from the hand that is blessed.

Seek The Lord

Oh seek the Lord,
You'd better hear me say,
Seek the Lord and live again someday,
you'll never bend your knee to pray,
if you don't choose the Lord's blessed way.
When people need saving
from Satan's enslaving,
to his snare they are always confined,
so why don't you go preaching,
and keep right on teaching,
saying "Satan get thee behind."
Oh work for him,
labor night and day,
work for Jesus and he will repay
work for Jesus and display,
that from him you'll never stray.

Drunk with Wine

Be not drunk with wine wherein is excess,
but be filled with the spirit of God and it's rest,
which excites the praise of God, the mouth which speaks,
to yourself in Psalms, hymns, and spiritual songs;
hark! Listen, for so I be quiet,
and taste of the melody in my heart to the priest,
which blesses us with Thanksgiving for all things complete,
and makes life worth living success one's defeat.

World Upside Down

Emerging from my house after April Showers,
mud holes and puddles affected my view.
I almost fell in - my head began to swim
as the depth of the puddle held the sky so blue.

Down in my puddle stood the tree upside down,
it's long arms reaching downward to the sky,
and waving to me, as the scene I did see,
were the leaves on the trees so high.

Lying on the bottom of my puddle,
was a figure I chance to see,
close scrutiny was given,
I found that figure was me.

My arms, my hair, my face to Bare,
lying in the bottom at the top of the sky,
and a Cloud floated by with billowy Grace,
to frame my face up there so high.

As I lay on the bottom at the top of the sky,
on flower beds of ease,
Bright Little Birds came floating by
three butterflies and honeybees.

Contentment is aloft, no matter the depth,
be it high or at the bottom of the sea,
make the best of the plan,
which comes to every man,
godliness with contentment is the key.

Great Rapidity

When to her came the Bliss of Heaven's kiss,
opening the gates of Heaven's fold,
then her voice was raised in glorious praise,
rending the depth of body and soul.

Then the virgin of old with a Heart full of gold,
erupted with Godly commitment,
hail to her friend, Elizabeth, then
Fanned and saluted her Kinsmen,
And out of her lips came Praise of whisper,
to confirm a message unfurled.
Heaven's rain came down,
with rejoicing sound,
a cloudburst from the glory world.

Mary's salutation Elizabeth heard,
a miraculous event was performed,
the angel said to me, though aged you may be
a son of six months is formed.

And it came to pass when Elizabeth heard the words,
of the future Mother of Our Lord,
leaped The Babe in her womb,
the Holy Ghost then soon filled her heart, soul,
body with a great Accord

Blessed art thou among women of mankind,
and blessed be the fruit of thy womb,
and whence is this to me that
the mother of my Lord, should be sent to me so soon.

Oh Sweet Deceit

How snug you lie in seclusion
decked with the ornament of Pious commitment,
an over cloak of laughter and love
that covers hands of passionate Spirits,
saintly and demonic from hell and heaven above.

Ah! Blissful deceit!
To hide behind a wall so protective,
though it be arrayed with Beauties rare,
with Grace Like Heaven and blessed words
that mischievously hides pretensive truth so bare,

Oh! Restful deceit!
To know a soul has been conquered,
with feigned words and dancing eyes,
while deep within a deceitful Soul,
a thousand demons abide.
To torture; to abuse; to molest;
Mankind's heart should be reposed in truthful rest

To veil action; to drape in Black;
a joyous heart of continual laughter,
a sad, sad soul, so you enact,
and all the while we have met the crafter.

Youth abides within a better heart no more,
for youth cannot be seen,
the lines upon the face are aged and hoary,
they present a pitiful tale of grief and woe.

Aloft

When mankind lifts his eyes aloft,
Integrious motives to prompt his thought
a smile of love from the face above,
enlightens the Mortal eye and heart.

When man inclines his heart on high,
Majestic robes enshroud him,
clouds of peace unearthly bliss,
cling round about him.

God frowns upon a wicked man,
Abominations prompt his action,
his ways are cursed,
childhood and birth,
for rejecting God's transaction.

A "Childhood" Profession

What ecstasy felt by Angelic host
at command of God to deliver the word
unto many the well-favored motherhood.

Transferring their emotions, their word did import
and stuck like a dagger The Virgin's Pure Heart.

The spiritual Joy left the Angels Above
descended like a cloak gentle as a dove,
and fell about Mary the one so beloved.

She magnified her Lord in holy and pure love,
to be chosen by the Holy Ghost to mother her Lord
so highly exalted by a noble estate
to birth her holy potentate.

Her heart swelled great with ecstasies there
the spirit like a river flows everywhere,
the trusted surrender to many come,
to refute every obstacle,
to Bear every blow that presented itself from Satan's
Convoy,
to condemn and rebuke and Endeavor to destroy.

God still finds his spirit in the heart of man
to give birth to a soul a new life to gain
the first born son being Jesus our Lord
we follow as it were in chronological Accord.

The holy writ declares "without natural affection"
many people have lost their desire for conception
that natural love and eager employ
forgetting the pain looking forward with joy
that a child should be born be it girl or boy.

This rare Joy is not too easily attained
for men have declined down the long strain
and have lost their desire for Godly possession
the laughter and love of a childhood profession.

The Upward Search

When I Said, "Please show me Heaven"
Please show me the streets of Gold.
Show me my father, my mother,
My sister, my brother,
And the saints
Of whom I am told.

Please show me the materials I am sending,
Be it hay, stubble, silver
or gold
for the great Builders fond
acceptance
though my labor be foul or four-fold.

Please show me
the grades I am making,
have my diligent tasks o'er shadowed my past?
Have my failures been underscored?

Have my
transgressions gone
on before
ere they Place me beneath
the sod?
To Blacken my way
or darken my day
and blot out my life with God?

Again I desired
the spiritual ways
of him and the Heavenly
Realm my answer?
No one can.

About the Author

Opal Busbee Staples was born on September 30, 1914 in West Texas. She was the youngest child of Henry Floyd Busbee and Ruby West Busbee. Her mother and father traveled with his work and each of the three siblings was born in a different state. They later divorced when Opal was very young. Henry Floyd took the three children and as a single working parent, had to put them in an orphanage in Memphis, TN at a very young age. Later they were placed in a Catholic Orphanage in Mobile, AL for a short period of time. He remarried and the children returned to Laurel and grew up in this area with their father, Henry and their stepmother, Frances Narcissis Rymes Busbee. Opal was on the basketball team during her high school years while staying in Brookhaven. She resided there with her Aunt Flossie and Uncle Fate Nations, Henry's sister and her husband.

In the year of 1937 on January 5, Opal and Victor Staples exchanged vows. They were married by a Justice of the peace. Victor grew up in and around Jones County. His father worked in the timber business which was booming in the early part of 1900. He did not talk a lot about his early years or his family. Victor was involved in high school sports and was the quarterback for the Clara High School Football team in 1929. He attended Jones Jr. College and later dropped out. This was during the depression and very few families could afford food and clothing, let alone a college education. Rose Ellen was the first child to come along on September 22, 1938. She was such a joy to the family.

On January 16, 1940, Gary Victor was born. He made his appearance at home on a snowy day. Dr. Boone was kind enough to make a home delivery. Early pictures show Gary very full of self. Rachel Louise was the third child. She was born August 25, 1941. She was a pretty little blonde. On April 12, 1943, Sarah Pauline joined Rose Ellen, Gary, and Rachel. Opal had four children in a period of 5 years. All were a happy family with the normal ups and downs of everyday living in the '40's. In December 1943, tragedy struck the family. Rose Ellen came down with diphtheria and died. This was devastating for the parents and it took many years for them to get past the heartaches of losing their oldest child. Granny Busbee lived next door and she was a big part of the family. There was a strong bond of love that entwined her daily life with the children until all were grown and she passed away. She was a step-grandmother and this made her love for the family even more special.

Rebecca Joy came along on September 5, 1944. Everyone said she looked just like Rose Ellen. Opal always thought she did and maybe this was a comfort to her. Opal was a saint. She was also a Trojan. In the next four years, four more children were born.

David Michael came along on April 3, 1946. When he was small, he could run very fast. If he thought he was going to get a switching, there was no one who could catch him. This might have laid the foundations for later years. He won the 880 yard run at the state track finals in 1963. Mary Judith was born on April 24, 1947. Everyone thought she would be the baby girl. John Timothy was born June 25, 1948 weighing in at 14 pounds. James Daniel was born July 25, 1949. He is the family chef. Victor was pastor for a small community church which had been started by Grandpa Busbee. Glade Pentecostal Church was a small church but when the Staples Family got there it was half-full. The family was raised to go to church at least 4 times a week and all went if healthy. The Staples were taught to respect God and country. Life in general centered round the church. The family met so many people from all walks of life there. Visiting evangelist and singers from across the country crossed the thresholds of the little church.

The singing Sullivan Family were frequent visitors as well as the child evangelist, Floy Marie Bell. All these people impacted life in a positive way. One night in 1958, little Joe was left at church. Somehow, he missed getting in the car. He had gone to sleep and when he awoke he started walking home alone. The home was located on Hwy 15 S about one and a half mile from the church. Someone stopped and gave him a ride home. He was about 6 years old. He has had a

Guardian Angel more than once in his lifetime. Jack Nathaniel was the next little fellow to come along. He is not a little one any longer. He is at least 6 ft 4 in tall and his weight suits his height. He was born March 3, 1951. Paul Joseph was born on June 27, 1952 (Joe was the one left at church). He was kind of small as a child. It was because Jack loved to share (or take) his bottle with him at mealtime, all the while patting him gently.

Benjamin Neil was born on February 14, 1954. Opal went to Boone Clinic with labor pains. It was Sunday and they sent her home around noon. Later that night Benjamin was born weighing in at 12 lbs. and some ounces. What a Valentine! Well, it was time for another girl. The next addition was Vicki Deborah born on March 16, 1956, a sweet little sister and loved dearly. It was nice to have a little girl for a change. The older ones took good care of her as if she were their own child. Sam was born on April 8, 1957. He was the last of the bunch. Opal was 44 years old and knew it was time for a break. A break – are you kidding? The house was usually filled with many friends and relatives. Opal cooked biscuits, about forty at one time. With such a large family, there was always interesting people around and exciting things happening. It would take the whole Staples Bunch each contributing their own unique memories to give a small glimpse of life with thirteen children at home. Ten children attended school simultaneously.

The entire family ate meals together. Getting ready for school, work, and church at one time with one bathroom was definitely a challenge. Life at the house with thirteen children could be hectic. It could be interesting. It could also be fun and exciting. You can rest assured it was a unique experience and a rare adventure. The family has been so blessed because of the heritage left behind. Living and interacting with so many siblings closely gave a jumpstart in life. It prepared and taught one how to work and live with other people in peace and good will. Some feelings are often bittersweet because the parents divorced in 1972. Victor passed away on February 8, 1994 and Opal died on April 24, 1997.

At the foundation of this gigantic family was a beautiful and loving lady. She was friendly and cordial to the visiting friends and ministers. A prayerful lady, she was always ready to minister to others while guiding the duties at home. Pregnant with 14 babies consumed much of her married life. A few miscarriages along the way drew her closer to Jesus as she walked through the "valley of the shadow of death" many times. The anointing of the Holy Spirit was present to heal, revive, and comfort her while raising family. This virtuous woman grew strong enough by the grace of God to survive the everyday battles of homemaking "one of the highest callings on earth given by God. "THANKS MOM FOR EVERYTHING"

www.ingramcontent.com/pod-product-compliance
Lightning Source LLC
Chambersburg PA
CBHW060806050426
42449CB00008B/1570